Love After The Riots

by

Juan Felipe Herrera

CURBSTONE PRESS

FIRST EDITION, 1996
Copyright © 1996 Juan Felipe Herrera

Printed in the U.S. on acid-free paper by BookCrafters
Cover design: Stephanie Church

Curbstone Press is a 501(c)(3) nonprofit publishing house whose
operations are supported in part by private donations and by
grants from ADCO Foundation, J. Walton Bissell Foundation,
Inc., Witter Bynner Foundation for Poetry, Inc., Connecticut
Commission on the Arts, Connecticut Arts Endowment Fund,
The Ford Foundation, The Greater Hartford Arts Council,
Lannan Foundation, LEF Foundation, Lila Wallace-Reader's
Digest Literary Publishers Marketing Development Program,
administered by the Council of Literary Magazines and Presses,
The Andrew W. Mellon Foundation, National Endowment for
the Arts-Literature, National Endowment for the Arts
International Projects Initiative and The Plumsock Fund.

Library of Congress Cataloging-in-Publication Data

Herrera, Juan Felipe.
    Love after the riots / by Juan Felipe Herrera. — 1st ed.
        p.   cm.
    ISBN 1-880684-28-4
    1. Man woman relationships—California—Los Angeles—Poetry.
2. Mexican Americans—California—Los Angeles—Poetry. 3.
Riots—California—Los Angeles—Poetry. 4. Love poetry, American.
I. Title.
PS3558.E74L68   1996
811'.54—dc20   95-52279

published by
CURBSTONE PRESS   321 Jackson Street   Willimantic, CT 06226
phone: (203) 423-5110   e-mail: curbston@connix.com
visit our WWW site at http://www.connix.com/~curbston/

Contents

7:30 pm /Thursday   9

7:35 pm   10

8:00 pm   11

8:35 pm   12

8.37 pm   13

8:45 pm   14

9:15 pm   15

9:20 pm   16

9:40 pm   17

10:00 pm   18

10:13 pm   19

11:00 pm   20

11:07 pm   21

12:01 am   22

12:02   23

12:04   24

1:03 am/Friday   25

1:04 am   26

1:06 am   27

1:08 am   28

1:15 am   29

1:33 am   30

2:00 am   31

2:05 am   32

2:09 am   33

2:11 am   34

2:13 am	35
2:37 am	36
2:40 am	37
2:47 am	38
2:59 am	39
3:03 am	40
3:07 am	41
3:09 am	42
3:11 am	43
3:27 am	44
3:45 am	45
3:58 am	46
3:59 am	47
4:15 am	48
4:21 am	49
4:44 am	50
4:48 am	51
5:00 am	52
5:03 am	53
5:07 am	54
5:14 am	55
5:17 am	56
5:18 am	57
5:30 am	58
5:37 am	59
5:53 am	60
5:57 am	61
6:01	62

Someone, perhaps, is alive. But we, here
absorbed in listening to the ancient voice
seek for a sign that outreaches life,
earth's dark sorcery
where even among the tombs of rubble
the maligned grass rears up its flower.

— Salvatore Quasimodo

It is right after supper,
when the wind smells of warm familial misery
lost in a thousand kitchens,
in the long, illuminated streets
spied on by brighter stars.

— Pier Paolo Pasolini

to Marga, to M. de las Flores, to M&M

Love After the Riots

7:30 pm / Thursday

Below the helicopter, running from the system.
Leaving L.A. Going with these whipping blades,
pulling over my face. They swarm into me,

bellow. In the name of Dante Alighieri;
follow his equestrian milk to the tenth ring,
ragged ivory.

Riot buildings held in orgasm,
circular wrestling, efficiencies
with our thighs that splash

waters of cinnamon guns;
this thief's oboe.

This new world
mechanical bedroom in the center of Ave. X
— outside, yes, there is
chalkdust & eighteen wheelers on fire.

7:35 pm

Marga Marylin: a Mexican blonde, pasted
with my Rollieflex. Throws molotovs
on Normandie Street. Soda bottles with bad juice
at the wavy curbs.

We steal a box of videos. Hi-density.

Pasted with the eyes askance.
When did I meet you?

When I came to you, she tells me,
reading my mind — caught up with telephone calls,
makeshift bandages, ready to burn
into the running-blade shadow. Escape? Yes.

8:00 pm

M&M
wears the green shirt of the golden Che.
She calls the head waiter at Porky's on Whittier.
We leave, we drink & trade notes
in the basilica.

Sweet serum in the gutters,
licorice transfusions.

We dance Balinese hulas,
swift gold and stiff masks of musk.

Out in the corridors, by the traffic ribbons
night youth still swagger & sell
their love dipped in Michaelangelo's hair.

She digs into me.
Nervous snails
on her bellybutton,
my tropical tongue.

8:35 pm

We examine the motion of cops
and their broken needles of orange light.

Can I ask her to dance? She pulls the point of my hair.
Below, a fat man in a penguin shirt
carries another man away from the restaurant.
I puff, raise my fingers — she

wants a word with me.
My Indian musical background.
Why? Someday he's gonna smash your face,
she says — her ex-husband, his nose,
his affairs.

8:37 pm

The facts are as follows: Marga steps down
with her dark glass.

She folds her hands and then she unfolds them.
The jazz band speaks her language
plays something by Miles;
Venus di Milo.

8:45 pm

Alone now, in the garage with bricks,
the streets are still hot with glass
and her determined voice.

Another sigh,
an island, a cigarette, too much bum money
& gas masks have gone into this.

We are both in the same straits. In South-Central.
Passolini spills into the riot. Nothing
but to look at her silk back,
her hands behind herself.

9:15 pm

When Can We Make Love?

This time a woman yells out
lightly from the roof above.
I 'll tell you her name.

Tumballa in a nurse's outfit, but
spiced with a taxi-driver's magic.
I dim the lights.
A waiter leaves on his motorcycle.

Play tumbao riffs
crackle the concrete, flying up.
Maracas, skull workers
in the background.

9:20 pm

Back up. Marga talks.
I drive against my best intentions.
Santa Monica, Venice — Albert King on the box.

By the sea & the vices of families
gone asleep in the smoke. 5000 lire
and she does not look at my face.

She says I look like Gregory Peck. The auto
swerves up the alley. She lives alone, now.

Stop for coffee. Read the Times Mirror.
Her skirt, my pants. The wheel stays
alone in the night shade. Silence,
a stone, tiny in her boot heel.

9:40 pm

Hear the footsteps. The flower shriek in my hand
sways the flood down the stairs.

We talk about the red sirens and wonder
about our tongues. I wonder.
In this apartment everything is possible.
Motorcycle-leather cops
turn the corner toward the piers.

Still, her glasses
make her look courteous and severe.
Lay down and smile. Move the cartoon
arms up with abandon, again. We embrace
against the boards.

Rodney King's handsome face
flashes through the curtain, flashes
across my forehead.

10:00 pm

Hot stripes down
my musical chest again. A kiss, a wave.
Pieces, pieces. Flannel, bras
autopsies & tobacco.

A moan from the next bedroom
in softness and Latino voices.
Someone falls. The TV scratches
without characters.

I drive back to see her,
up the stairs. The whiteness blinds me.
What happened? Arrests, they say.

10:13 pm

The phone sucks
my ear with her melody. Who
can take care of this, of her?
Next time she'll die. The TR-3 tumbles
down the avenues to the clinic.

11:00 pm

(Again), a nun talks about
politics to her receptionist. Please.
Go right in. Here, right in.
By the lamp,
by the steel-ringed bedpan.

Outside a hospital
Inside a hospital.
The careening asphalt swerves into science.

11:07 pm

Kiss her. Marga will leave shortly,
again with the towel wrapped around her belly.
I whimper in her hands, turn my head
and reach for her face. Talk to the wall,

pace with the nun,
the Sister with her canonical headdress.
She was throwing something
that burned her hands, the nun says.

The bell rings in dire seriousness.
The men, the young men
with cameras, arrive.

A report is being hustled away
under the tripod.

12:01 am

Marga is here now,
in furs and blondish beeps.
Her cape turns back into the car.
A wry kiss again to the tiny public.

We are ready to emerge. Is this city
ready to breathe — in flames?
I am swollen with glassy air.

How is this possible? Who are the stars
of the production underway?
Spike Lee's film journal ruffles
in the back seat.

Call me Pinal; I tell her
this was a long time ago.

12:02

They call her Mariana Carnación.
They call me John Orizaba. Next
to the mad mountain, to a concave bedlam.

The bassoon at the Sherwin Williams paint store
blows its blackness into the void—sky
comes up with a trio of violins.

We can hardly move down the parade,
down the walkways; Oprah Winfrey in the pressroom.

Madame, the reporter asks. Madame.
How long will you be staying in Rome?

12:04

Another vested cop
welcomes me.

Please, he laughs. More cameras.
A see-through blouse. Cannelloni, two drops
of French perfume. The asses ask
epistemological questions about Justice.

The Mayor is not in the tour.

(I am alone with her — an overgrown hippie,
the reporter said. He swings his breasts
when he says this.)
She swings her shoulders. Lucille Montiel
another reporter calls
on the phone, behind quarters.

1:03 am / Friday

Marga speaks of ingredients. Do you really
love me, she asks me. My illusions
take me far, up here, in Chinese music,
tassels. Come and look, up the stairs
again in muffled laughter, behind the church.
The best place for delicacy.

Cameras keep getting in the way.
Arched windows, baroque. Giotto drags a stiletto,
an embroidered cape, & cannot be seen
through the fire engines.

1:04 am

I am out of film. Where has she gone?
The convex, the tiny seat. Her hand by the bells,
the howling bells crossed with light
and crowd music, gold swirls in my head,
the shadow of the stairs, up again,
so many stairs and apartments,

eyeglasses & shattered screens, bread slices of tin,
an upturned Mercedes below her, below me, O Florence
O Los Angeles?

1:06 am

Marga's hat blows away with the smoke
of a distant clarinet, another skull on fire. We embrace
again and dance, we dance, especially
we dance. In the twelfth ring.

The flames, the maracas and her pursed lips
save me. This first day of creation.

The devil lays the piano
with Mozart's green eyes.
We will go back to America one day,
with her boa, whitish — Pinal
behind her.

1:08 am

I must see you alone.

A man's fair chest gets in the way
as she screams. It's Giotto. What
is he doing here? This divine actor.

Her throaty voice and laughter, now
his Cha Cha Cha arms up through her
tresses. Night.

What is he doing here?
"Do you like my sexy beard, kid?" he asks her.
He pulls her away and they dance.
Sax man save me, save me sax man.

1:15 am

It must be the evil of my eyes,
simply. Ambulances.

I haven't forgotten that I work tomorrow.
Marga talks to the jazz guitarist.
With my hand, I tell her
it was first rate. More wine please.

Escusi uno momento,

I stumble as usual,
elegant and simplistic, while
the audience shouts for an r&r piece
by Little Richard;
an accent from California with
thick microphones from the fifties.

1:33 am

Cuban shirts and slick blueness.
A wire hangs down my vest, blowing by the floor.
My own scars. Humming destructions
to myself. Her voice.

"Get ready," the stretched rocker sings
as we move out to an alley and swerve,
rub our clothes and skin.

She is spinning above my shoulders.
Music is the first concession a rebellion allows,
she tells me in her marked accent.

Bravisimo. "Dangerous
but beautiful, Madame," the waiter says.

2:00 am

That's fine, I say.
You can always say that in the scene.
Marga runs away again.
Or am I running away again?

I leave it to you and the boa,
the TR-3 and its stoic devotions.
Where is she going now?

2:05 am

Next stop, rivets sizzle.
The road looms. With men, she says,
with grayness.

The short mirror
at the chrome top reminds me —
you cannot go back.

We stop and rest with the cricklets.
She opens the door while I pull
myself up with the windshield.

Maracas again. This time
with the shiver of news cameras,
a million feet of videotape.
Swivel to the rap-beats.

2:09 am

Marga, yes?
Her eyes, a smile again
the ruffled boa — calling someone,
she says.

Someone out there, in the new rubble
office. See it, Pinal?

Now we are apart.

She howls back. I howl back.
A cigarette. The night slips through my thighs.
A helicopter whirls.

2:11 am

At the tiny restaurant:
    Fiore Escavatrice

Antipasto.
We are always together,
she says. Antipasto — this
is how we begin our conversations.

Pinal, she says, with her wide
and perfect smile, her Mexican elegance.

We talk about our fathers.
A jagged tree appears outside.
Stings me.

2:13 am

Marga picks up a kitten.
Runs. Fire again,
it comes so quickly in Los Angeles,
in this Italian tavern.

But this is Rome. Can't be Rome.
It is. Marga & me. We are bound

to a Purgatorio of Margas & Pinals,
of kittens resting their tiny paws
on the fountain,

the waters' flowing,
of four million Marga's & Pinals
face up with Montale, face
in the Caracalla baths, oil
sweat, juice, and broken pianos.

2:37 am

Bathing, I sit back foolish &
forlorn, with my wristband knotted.
Sing to her.

We are pasted together, a new form,
by duck blood, by asphalt & dog blood
by smoke & skull maracas, by a foreign rhythm
of sax, tumbao & sex.

2:40 am

The bath water stops & fades.
Everything stops & fades.

The lions of basalt and marble slime
float under her small feet.

Rome sparkles by the flames
of the Harbor Freeway.

A camera flashes across
South-Central L.A.

2:47 am

Pinal,
I am wearing a striped dress —
velveteen, full-blown by spring.

The colonnades, the Caracalla baths
where Pasolini raced a blue Ducati, the pews
where they strung me up for confession.

Mea culpa
Mea culpa
Mea culpa

It doesn't matter now. Too many light years
behind my boa. Sanskrit grammar.

Turn up the heat now.
Turn it up so you can read it, she says.

2:59 am

Marga has dissolved.
Into another scene.

I look down at my tie.
Red blotches sprouting from my arms.
Twisted on the asphalt —
bricks and televisions,
electric holes of popped bread.

3:03 am

The TR-3 spins at 75 kilometers.
Florence Street, an egg. Eat, she says.

Photographers?
Yes, only for you, she says.
Eat it, she says in Italian.

We go by the country,
a miracle is in the making.
People are running.

Where are the children? A scoop
about the raped women in Bosnia.
Their elongated scarves are the clues,
Marga whispers into my tiny ear.

3:07 am

Seven black children are being held hostage
by the vested cops. A Korean, an Arab, a Mexican with a broom.
Bicycles and an umbrella with an old woman.
Upside down, she struggles for her face.

No one can go home now. America,
America.

A grandfather man comes out of the building.
That's it, the reporter shouts
and sings Ave Maria.

3:09 am

Marga's Axiom:
Five Pavarottis are necessary
to make the world turn one centimeter.

3:11 am

I am wearing a sleeveless.
She is floating.

O, Asphalt Madonna. Marga pleads
to the sky, mouth a twist of bluish cloud.

Who is directing your film?
Who is responsible?

A man with an artificial tree walks by.
A thin boy prays to the tree
by the TR-3 tires.

Night lamps
sizzle with peasant songs.
An Army sign lights up.

3:27 am

A huge crowd has gathered, curious.
More reporters, massed, the sky
clear in the night,
in the custody of slaughter.

They say the Blessed Virgin has appeared.
They have always said this.

Saw her in San Antonio Padua.
I moved over to her & prayed,
a tall wavy candle in my hands,
tears down her seductive ceramic eyes.

A reporter climbs the scaffold to its triangular point,
by the spotlight on a webbed cloud. Marga walks
long steps by a foreign ambulance truck.

3:45 am

She asks them what are you doing
to put the fires out?
I know she is asking me.

Praying too.

She says
something like this:
A torch, a line of torches, men
in plumber uniforms, in laundry jackets,

a blackened sky with a little boy & girl rustling
their feet in the silk. A vigil. Floating pillows,
crushed bed posts, open night-cream jars.

3:58 am

Marga is down there somewhere.
Twelve thousand characters,
the gong of the light, the smoke,
shards. Pouring now.

They've taken shelter in the bus.
Marga's real name is Flavia, she says.

They are holding hands. The crowd keeps
something hidden — going mad, cameras
in the night air. But the smoke crashes

through the rubber canopies, the plastic caps.
So we run.

3:59 am

There is no church here, there will not be one.
A little girl cries & they take her away.
I am far from the restaurant. Only stubs,
flower stems and pipes come up.

I open my bag for water.
You've no right to do this,
Marga screams at a reporter, at the vested man
with a camera, coming closer to her.
The horns blast. They are leaving
in zig-zag routes, buses and more umbrellas.

4:15 am

The man that came for a cure has died.
He came from the villages, for the healing.
The wrap is on the ground & prayers,
instead of rain, come down;

the sky spotted
with inappropriate parishoners.

Yodeling rich men
and women. No one speaks Italian,
no one speaks American.

4:21 am

Just love yourself, she says.
Strum your Indian lute, don't argue about me.
Other words:

mysterious,
maternal,
original,
tiger. These are not the words.

Something about you & me &
this shattered basilica.

Body? Soul? Permit me, this is Pinal.
This is loss, the reporter says,
something that can't make love.

4:44 am

I tell him, all colors.
I've written this before in important books.

Optimism and faith, constant surprises
like Fellini recommends.

Mirrors are bad, he says. Taxis are good.
Remember. Leave nothing to chance —
the How-Can-I-Exist.

Beware of imprisonment, remain free,
the matron with the parasol on the burning couch says.

4:48 am

I've read this poetry before. Unlike me.
A living, clear, honest style with subterfuge.

It may happen tomorrow. To live intensely,
in spiritual fulfillment. Marga almost falls
back when I get to fulfillment
on the way to miracle.

Fire drenched
with voices of fire. An American just
walked in and talks about masculine uncertainty,

about quality. What all Americans ponder
in the time of destruction.
Something more stimulating than jazz, he says.

5:00 am

Poetry. On charcoals.

A Neruda with a Crane.

A child dressed in Berryman's pajamas.

You'll catch a cold first,

then you'll laugh & sit down.

You'll speak in Italian like M&M.

My native language. *Oscuro, tuto felice.*

See? Lovely music, *bella.*

Say goodnight. Kiss, kiss. Marga.

Combinations of words, expressions

fascinate her.

5:03 am

I agree.

Another phrase from the rich,
the invisible rich, dawdling in Beverly Hills.

They are saying Giotto & Montale
brought this on themselves, that Rome
burns because the peasants
did not worship correctly. They
are holding up the videotape against the moon.
They read it out loud in polished accents.

They are invisible now.

Ask the Devil-dog, Marga tells them. Ask.
Examine my DNA.

5:07 am

Just realize this & look away. Look up,
over yonder. A blackened Matisse —
a hot pink cut-out floats into Hollywood.

The new spirit.

5:14 am

Caught again without a cigarette,
my slackened muscles, detached,
slide under my shirt, grasping for lies
& truths and losses and desires.

Call Marga again with an organ
roaring in the background.

5:17 am

I want to see Fellinni.
Ask him these questions:

How to sing lalalalalalalalalala?
How to eat here?
How to pray in the basilica?
How to travel through this candid broken Rome ?
How to be here?
How to pronounce Annunzio?
How is my father, is he tapping his cane?
How do you cry and then turn around?
Have you heard this before?
Where is Gradiska?
Where is Nino?

5:18 am

Standing alone in the fullness
of Sebastian Bach in Cuba, I scramble
for her telephone, again
in my Triumph. Not Pinal, maybe Jo-Jo,
my brother, in his swing suit when we climb
the walls at the night parlour with Marga,
napkins full of love and juice.

The heat keeps rising,
never cools. It's artistic this way,
swallowed back by the umber soul.

5:30 am

We've nothing to do. Even with the wars,
even with the mobius strip of bodies
tied to me and you, we've nothing to do.
Bring your friend, Sylvia. Bring her lover, Lo.
Bring yourself, Marga. Jump into
the Triumph with spoke rims,
let's get best suckers & meet the reporter.

Meet the naked flames dressed as lovers
in one-hundred-and-eighteen thousand characters.
More drinks to quench the trenches, the glitter
of the military caps and tilted blouses.

5:37 am

This is all I have. A bottle of ink
for my marriage. Who is ordering?
Who is shaking their shoulder? Sweet shoulders
of lovemaking. Toast. For you,
for me. Yes, Yes.

The piano dreams & the waiter brings
a bottle. Please don't get up, he says.
America. Italy. Like twin halos.

Shh. The reporter is here with a sad suit,
with mascara above his dimples.

I toast to you. The balloon snaps and
Marga laughs.

The old man next to me opens his mouth
and drinks with me. *Bene bene.*

He holds his forehead.
Tropical dizziness down the breastbone.

5:53 am

They don't dance like this anymore,
the old man says. He watches
me write to the string bass beat.
In the alley it's time to go.
In good company. Speeding.

When I was a teenager
I dreamed of Volvos & stormy windows,
she whispers.

5:57 am

Marga runs. I walk.
This is a respectable building, she tells me.
Up the stairs. Get the boa.
It's nothing. The whistle beats over the stove
near the bed. It's nothing, The phone rings.

In the next room Marga massages her feet.
This is Rome at the end of the century. Still, 6:00 am:
the time when lovers wake up in sweat,
wanting to believe in something, unstrapped fire —
anything besides the hotel, besides the gibberish.

6:01

Write to me. Marga.
The black taxi leaves plainly.
Two men fight the way men fight when
they are clumsy and wonderful. Cowards.
Next car.

I can go to bed now. My brother is away.
I mumble another place, buildings with ragged windows.
Collared shirts, a little boy with a burning cane,
a painting of Hollywood in the forties.
A sports car with fog lights, the wet streets.

CURBSTONE PRESS, INC.

is a non-profit publishing house dedicated to literature that reflects a commitment to social change, with an emphasis on contemporary writing from Latin America and Latino communities in the United States. Curbstone presents writers who give voice to the unheard in a language that goes beyond denunciation to celebrate, honor and teach. Curbstone builds bridges between its writers and the public – from inner-city to rural areas, colleges to community centers, children to adults. Curbstone seeks out the highest aesthetic expression of the dedication to human rights and intercultural understanding: poetry, fiction, testimonies, photography.

This mission requires more than just producing books. It requires ensuring that as many people as possible know about these books and read them. To achieve this, a large portion of Curbstone's schedule is dedicated to arranging tours and programs for its authors, working with public school and university teachers to enrich curricula, reaching out to underserved audiences by donating books and conducting readings and community programs, and promoting discussion in the media. It is only through these combined efforts that literature can truly make a difference.

Curbstone Press, like all non-profit presses, depends on the support of individuals, foundations, and government agencies to bring you, the reader, works of literary merit and social significance which might not find a place in profit-driven publishing channels. Our sincere thanks to the many individuals who support this endeavor and to the following foundations and government agencies: ADCO Foundation, Witter Bynner Foundation for Poetry, Inc., Connecticut Commission on the Arts, Connecticut Arts Endowment Fund, Ford Foundation, Lannan Foundation, LEF Foundation, Lila Wallace-Reader's Digest Fund, The Andrew W. Mellon Foundation, National Endowment for the Arts, and The Plumsock Fund.

Please support Curbstone's efforts to present the diverse voices and views that make our culture richer. Tax-deductible donations can be made to Curbstone Press, 321 Jackson Street, Willimantic, CT 06226.
phone: (203) 423-5110   e-mail: curbston@connix.com
visit our WWW site at http://www.connix.com/~curbston/